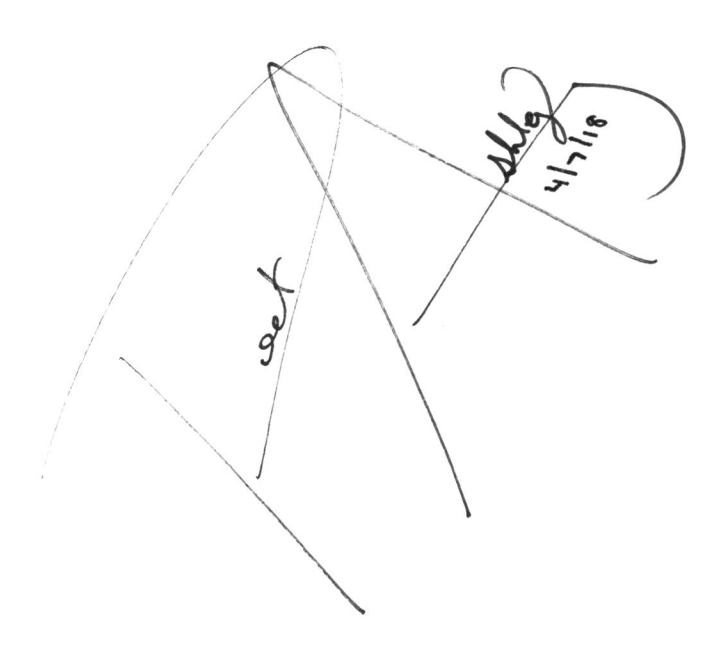

Chains are Broken
Poems of Prayer

by Poet Ashley J

Published by TEAM PUBLICATIONS LLC
Brenda Hill, Editor-in-Chief
Cecely Clark, Editor
Tracy Clark, General Manager Lake Charles, LA 70605

Text ©2017 by Poet Ashley J

Cover Art © 2017 Leroy Tademy Jr.
Tademy Photography
www.tademydandp.com

Book Design: Laurie Barrows
LaurieBarrows.com

ISBN -13: 978-0-9969009-3-5

This book or parts thereof may not be reproduced in any form,stored in a retrieval system, or transmitted in any form by any means-electronic, mechanical, photocopy, recording, digital,or otherwise-without prior written permission of the author and illustrator, except as provided by United States of America copyright law.

Printed in the United States of America

Published in the United States of America

Unless otherwise indicated, scripture quotations are from the King James Version of the Bible.

Library of Congress Cataloging-in-Publication Data
Johnson-Montegut , Ashley, 1990

Acknowledgments:

First, I must give thanks to God for blessing me with life and gifts. I give thanks to my mother, Karen Magee, for giving me birth to live the life God gave to me. "Mama, you helped me become the woman I am today and I love you. You were always there, supporting me, when I needed you the most." I give thanks to my amazing husband, Paul Montegut, who supported me through my whole journey. He is the ear that listens to my material before I present it to others. I give thanks to my sister, Tiffanie Johnson, for constructive conversations that helped me strive to do better. To my manager, Karen "Nikki" Green, "Thank you for believing in my gifts and helping me reach my goals and dreams." A special thanks to Karen Collins, my God-sent friend, for inspiring me to write this book and helping me to grow spiritually. A final thanks to my best friend, Ebony Meche, all the rest of my family members, church members, co workers, and many others who inspired me on my journey. I love each and every one of you. In some ways, my *Chains are Broken* because of you!

Introduction

God created us and placed us in the womb of 'Woman.' We call her 'Ma', 'Mom,' 'Mother,' etc. We come here pure and innocent, but we do not stay that way for very long. Our daily challenges seem to be how we permit the world to rock us in its arms, place a stronghold on us and mold us into its image. We become attached and cannot let go of some things we have encountered along the way. We begin to feel imprisoned and on lock down. Freedom denied!!

I was guilty too!

As a little girl, I was a "sweet angel." God designed me perfectly! The more days I experienced in this world, the more bruises I received from the 'hurts of life.' I did not quite know how to handle these unwanted and painful life experiences until I accepted God in my life. Prayer was my answer.

Chains are Broken is a book of my poems of prayer that helped me escape worldly chains that left me feeling locked in spiritual cages. Possibly, you as well. It is designed to help you listen to my thoughts of struggles and gains and hear my heart."

Take off the orange jumpsuit donated to you by society! Put on the wardrobe of Jesus to break the chains over your life! Expand your mind and desires to seek and *embrace the world of God through His Son Jesus the Christ, our Lord and Savior! Desert the world of man-made ways!* "Reject Free-Dumb! Choose Freedom!

Table of Contents
Prayers — 1
Morning Prayer — 2
I Rise — 6
My Pledge — 8
In This Season — 9
Crying Out — 10
A Blessing You Are — 12
What's Ahead — 15
This Little Light of Mine — 17
Family Prayer — 20
Patience for a Friend — 22
Prayer of the Night — 25
Gifts — 28
The Unknown — 30
Closer — 32
But God — 35
God So Loved — 39
Fill Me Up — 41
Love Me — 44
Beauty For Ashes — 46
Starts With U-N-I — 50
All Souls Matter — 52
Earthly Dad — 55
I'm Intoxicated — 58
Trapped — 62
Take it to Your Sister — 65
Healing — 68
Living in Silence — 70
I'm That You — 76
Put a Period — 78
Surrender — 82
Right on Time — 85
Shadows of Death — 87
Found in the Pages — 90
Transformation — 93
Remodel — 96
Worship With No Regrets — 99
This is How I Sleep — 101

Poems 107
Many Questions	108
Give In	110
Run to God	112
One Man's Journey, Another Man's Lifestyle	115
Chains Are Broken	119
Loved One, Lost One	124
Unbroken Bond	127
There Could Never Be Just One Thing	130
I Met a Man	133
You Are The Man	136
HE IS…Someone to Talk About	138
Social Media	142
Be Who God Made	146
Wonderfully Made	148
My Identity	152
Confidentiality	157
Ebony	159
Coffee Girl	163
Open Your Book	167
Free-Dumb	171
Unity	175
God Is Not Man	178
Over It	181
Heart of Excuses	183
It Takes Two	187
Trigger of the Gun	190
Life Sentence	192
Shattered Glass	195
Seen a Demon	200
Put My Name On It	203
Salvation	205

Journal Pages 208

Prayers

Morning Prayer

Father,
Thank You,
Another morning You blessed me to see
Eyes are widening,
Loosening the crust from when I was sleeping

Thank You,
For allowing me to get out of bed
Standing firm on my two feet
Arms wide open
Stretching
Reaching for more of You
In desperation for Your help
Needing You to guide me, God

Lord, I pray to You
Begging You to open my eyes every morning
Not just for sight
Lord, give me vision

Empower my mind to fight
Flesh versus spirit
Give me the vision of the righteous,
The power to seek You
Even in the depths of the waves in Your ocean

As I understand it,
Sight is one form of vision
Meaning one piece
And I can't shortchange You
Lord,
You deserve for me to seek You wholeheartedly

I'll give You all of me
Expand my sight
So I can see You clearly
Sight, eyes
Vision, mind
Lord, come to me in every thought I think

You may be unseen to me
But You are not hidden
I may not physically see You
But I can feel Your presence

I pray not to lust over the things of the world
Instead, let my soul be attracted to You
Intrigued by Your creativity

You are larger than life
Lord never let me forget who You are
Let me be obedient
And listen to Your word

2 Corinthians, 4:18 tells me:

"While we look not at the things which are seen, but at the things which are not seen: for the things which are seen are temporal; but the things which are not seen are eternal."

Lord that tells me

You are forever

As I go through this day

I pray,

I can break every chain that prevents our intimacy

Let me become so anxious for You that when I am without You,

I suffer from anxiety

No prescription meds, no antidepressants

You are my pharmacy

Prescribing

Drugs of hope

Drugs of faith

Drugs of love

Drugs of compassion

Drugs of the capability of You

Lord,

Thank You for whatever You have in store for this day

Let me walk in my purpose

And not keep reliving the trauma from all of my accidents

Lord,

Please bless this day ahead
In Jesus name,
Amen.

I Rise

In this hour
I come to You, Lord
In this minute
In this very second
I am calling on You, Lord

Father,
I ask
That You remove any contamination from my life
Asking You to raise me up
To be a better wife
I am not perfect
But I strive
My flesh may be weak
But I rise

I rise
Because You gave me a lift
You are my push
You are my gift

You are the Creator of my story
Every word of my sentence
You keep it 100
You are the realest

You are my tongue
You are my vocalist
You are my thoughts
You are my novelist,
The writer of my book
That has not been fairly read
Do not judge a book by its cover
Leave negative comments unsaid

I heard words will never hurt me
Actually they do sometimes
But I know You can take the pain away
Because You do it every time

My Pledge:

I promise to love like You love
I will be strong and courageous
Because I believe,
You are with me wherever I go
I know I can do all things through You,
You strengthen me
I will not just speak Your word
But it, I will show
I will hide Your commandments in my heart
I will not put another god before You,
Whether it's a person, money, shoes, are clothes
I will treat others how I want to be treated
I will honor my mother and my father
Out of all things,
I will do everything in my power to put You first
I will have the confidence to stand firm on Your word
And let nothing turn me away from Your church
I will love my enemies
And I will turn the other cheek if need be
I will live my life as a Christian woman
Helping to build Your kingdom

In This Season

I am on Your plane
Up in the air
Without knowing where You are taking me
Like a woman blindfolded
Surprised and anxious to discover
Where we are landing

This season,
For the first time
I feel Your blood
Flowing in the lines of my veins
Something is about to take place
Move me
To the speed of your pace

Lord,
I don't know what You are doing in this season
I just ask,
You do not do it without little ol' me
I want to stay ready
So I will not have to worry about getting ready
Whatever this season brings
Let me be ready to receive

Crying Out

Father,
This world is dying
Man is corrupt
People are crying
Crying out for something
They just don't know for what

They are starving
Taking in anything that gets near
Even things that are not of You
Let them be cautious
About what they consume
I ask that you guide their feet to You

Father,
Be with my niece and nephews
As they grow up in this world,
Let them be covered with Your Son Jesus,
Dripping with His Blood

They may be babies right now
But give them understanding of who You are
Give me the tools to show up
To be the push they need to build a relationship with You
That will take them far

Father,
I know You are there
Because You are omnipresent
Where I go,
I'll take You along
Don't want Your appearance to go absent

I will tell the world You are here
I am not going to hide You
Or be ashamed,
Every place we go together
Just know, I am glad You came

A Blessing You Are

Dear God,
Lately my prayers have been selfish
Only asking for personal blessings
For me and my family
However, today
What I want to tell You is that I love You

Simple
Love You for being God
I am not worthy of You
But You make me feel high as the sky
Blue, downright beautiful

You are my best friend
When I have an issue
You are quick to listen
You do not shut me off
You do not make me feel stupid
Instead, You enlighten me
Keep reminding me of who You are
Just in case I forget
You bring the light bulb
When the atmosphere gets dim
You are more than amazing

Words cannot be found to describe You
Even in a dictionary
There will never be an accurate vocabulary
Yet, it does not mean I cannot try
I'll fish in the sea
Pulling out whatever gets hooked to the line
I am giving You the best description that comes to mind

Father,
To know You is an honor,
A blessing within itself
You allowed me to be the ambassador
Telling the world about Your Son Christ Jesus
Of how He will soon be back

Time to get the house in order
Starting now
Cannot wait
I do not want to have a surprised look on my face
When he shows up
As if it was unexpected company
Putting myself in a bad position
Talking like,
"Excuse my house"
(Like it hasn't always been in that condition)

Lord You are Savior

Protector

Creator

Lord of lords

King of kings

God of gods

I thank You because You are everything

A blessing from up above

What's Ahead?

I am calling on Thee
This morning,
Shall I see SONshine?
Beaming through the day
Shall I see clear, blue sky?
Or will there be clouds today?

I want to know what's ahead
Geared up
I am ready
For whatever
You may bring

I am calling on Thee
This morning,
Shall I see SONshine?
Beaming through the day
Shall I see clear, blue sky?

What lies before me?
My eyes cannot reach,
What's behind me?
My eyes squint,
No longer can they see

My past,
Passed me by
Myself,
I know longer recognize

I have been rerouted
I have been redeemed
Got a roommate
God lives inside of me

I am calling on Thee
This morning,
Shall I see SONshine?
Beaming through the day
Shall I see clear, blue sky?
Or will there be clouds today?

I want to know what's ahead
Geared up
I am ready
For whatever
You may bring

This Little Light of Mine

That light
That shines so bright,
In the midst of the air
Shine down on me
Lord, I know You are there

As I inhale,
A breath of fresh air
Lord let Your light shine on me,
Sprinkle Your blessings
In the interior of my soul
Lord, behold!

Lord, I come to You
Seeking for strength
Lord be with me
Today until the end

Hold tight to my body
Lord never let me go
When I do wrong,
Pull me in close
Lord do not give up on me
Especially,
Those times in the middle of the night
Where I cry alone

Lord, shine Your light on me
For I am just flesh
Weakened
Been broken
Lord, I am like a puzzle
Scattered all over
Needing to be put back together

Can we just cuddle for a second?
Maybe an hour
A day or two
Lord, I need You

You are the only one I can call on
In the middle of the night,
When everyone else is asleep
Smothered by their pillows

Lord I can call on You
And never get the answering machine
I can pray to You
You relay your message to me directly
That is why I can call on You

Lord, let me just do right in Your sight
I may struggle
I realize sometimes

I may not do exactly what You want me to do
I know I will sin
But Lord, let me not die in my sins
Let me repent
Fix wherever I am broken

Lord You are that light I will never turn off
I can keep You on all day long
And not worry about how high my light bill will be
Nor have to figure out the best bundle that saves me money
Lord, You are a package
A package I get for free
I will never return You
So I rip up and throw away my receipt

Family Prayer

Our Father,
Who is in heaven,
We surrender to You
Casting away the filth from the world
Replacing it with You

Can You hear our cry?
Do You even care?
Are we wasting our time?
Or, are You really there?

Father we need You
Sometimes we fall short
We call on You
For Your strength to pick us up

Bond our family
Do not let us grow apart
Let us show love
Let it be genuine from the heart

Bless our family
Heal our spirits
Cover us with the blood
Of Your Son Jesus

Give us shelter
In the time of a storm
Give us hope
When there is none

Give us peace in destruction
Let us have joy
Let us get along
Sharing and not being selfish
Provide us with a happy home

Construct us to be Holy
Remove any wickedness
We may have consumed
Purify us
Heal any emotional wounds

Can You hear our cry?
Do You even care?
Are we wasting our time?
Or, are You really there?

Patience for a Friend

God,
I'm coming to You on behalf of a friend
Asking for patience right now, Father
In the name of Jesus
I pray You allow her to parent like You parent her,
You are the supplier
Almighty God
You give chances after chances

She left You,
But You never disappeared from her, Father
She was disobedient, unfaithful, distasteful, Lord
Yet, You love her despite of it all

I thank You, Lord
I ask that she do for her kids
Exactly what You have done for her
Never let her give up on them
Let her remain mother and not their friend,
Merely fitting in with today's society

Bring showers of roses upon her
So she can pour all the love in her seeds,
Sounds of patience
Give her pretty pleases

With cherries on top
Give her hearts of compassion
Feet of faith

Let her walk on in the impossible,
Walk in her purpose
Give her grace
Opening gates
Moving mountains of heartbreaks and confusion

Father,
Let her break chains of redundancy
Make her washing machine full
Where she refuses to go through another cycle,
Unable to carry another load

Generation after generation
Picks up what they are taught
But Father,
Bless her with new ears, new lips, and a new heart

Catch her in time
Making her a better example for her children
Let them gain discipline
Breaking the cycle

You said,

If she gets close to You
You will draw near
I believe You will do what You say
So today,
I pray
You allow her to get closer with patience
Allow her to overcome any obstacles headed her way
Lord please,
Save her with amazing grace

Prayer of the Night

God,
You did it once again
Blessed me through this day
Kept me safe as if I were confidential
Hide me from evil
You reveal to me my gift
Letting me see my potential

Thank you
For keeping me strong in the storm of ignorant people
Luke 23:34 was my constant reminder
Where Jesus said,
"Father, forgive them, for they know not what they do."
Lord I come to You
Head bowed, heart humble, in full submission to You
Asking for forgiveness for the people,
Forgiveness for me too
For we are not perfect
But let us strive to be more like You

Lord,
They tried to kill my spirit
Isaiah 54:17 says,
"No weapon that is formed against thee shall prosper"
They tried but they were so unsuccessful

Thank You Father for strength of endurance
Thank You for patience
Thank You for assurance
Lord, I can thank You all night
For You are,
A Holy God,
Amazing in every way, shape, and form

Thank You for giving me a peace of mind
Thank You for being an on time God
For You are always on time
Thank You for blessing me with an incredible life partner
Thank You for my family, friends, and church members
Thank You Father for life itself
For You gave Your only Son
So we could have a chance to live
And I thank You

Father,
As I lay my head down to rest
I ask that You watch over me throughout the night
Protect me as I sleep
Protect my family
Be with the world as a whole
For it is out of order
Trying to run without You
But at the end,

They will regret the fact that they ran
I pray for peace
In Jesus name,
Amen.

Gifts

My mother always wondered,
What is her gift?
That one thing she enjoys
And is successful in

Searching through the list
She realized,
Singing, preaching, or performing
Isn't one of them

She continues to search
Only to find nothing
But then again
She may be looking in the wrong stack
There is more than one group of presents

Nothing just falls in your lap
Gifts come in different packages
Some are in gift bags
Some are wrapped
Some are easier to see then others
But elusiveness does not mean it is not there

Gift is God's Interesting way to Free us through Talent
Enlarging hearts for the abandon

Some gifts are just having compassion
Being that ear to others' story
A gift wrapped in uniqueness

Gifts are not just talents presented on a stage platform
The most beautiful things are performed back stage
Giving in a deeper way
Than anything ever imagined

Father,
Let her not be blinded by her purpose
But let her go out and do what you have chosen
And embrace it

Mother,
I'm praying for you
Asking God to give you understanding
To enlighten your mind to the hidden gift
Everything that goes up
Eventually starts landing

The Unknown

Do not worry about the unknown
God has it under control
Do not worry about friendships ending
Sometimes God has something else
Better in store

Sometimes what we think is sunshine
It is actually a cloud
Standing in the way
Of our clear, blue sky

Sometimes we hold on to people,
Who God is trying to release
We panic
Do not know what is happening
Falling to our knees

But do not worry about the unknown
God has it under control
We tend to doubt him
Why?
I just do not know

Father,
Someone is going through a storm

Going through the loss of someone
Dead or they may have just moved on
But either way,
It hurts

Sometimes we outgrow our loved ones
The journey we are on,
They are nowhere near close
But give us the mindset to keep pushing forward
Not letting anyone stop our flow

Yet, encourage them to follow the rhythm of your boat
Paddling to your promised land
I want to see what is in store
The unknown is usually scary
But I know it will be quite a surprise
I give it to You God
From Your water,
We will never sink
All we can do is rise

Closer

James 4:8

Draw near to God and He will draw near to you. Cleanse your hands, you sinners; and purify your hearts, you double-minded.

Jesus,

Thank You for Your Blood,

Thank You for your sacrifice,

You bled and died on the Cross

You gave me a chance at life

Jesus,

Help me to hear Your voice

Let me better distinguish

Picking the right choice,

Help me to spiritually grow inches

First learning Your voice

Renew me mentally

Lord, I can no longer be double-minded

Either I am a metaphor or a simile,

Either I am high in the sky for You

Or deceiving,

Lying like Satan do

I choose You

So I draw near

Knowing You will come closer too,
No hesitation, no fear
Looking forward, not toward the rear
Not worried
Knowing I have You

I am coming closer Lord,
I promise not to draw away,
I am still
My feet in place
My heart does race
Anxious to see the things You will do for me
Once I get closer

My youth was lost
Now I am older
Ex-anger sufferer,
Use to blow up instantaneously
Now I can keep my composure

Hands in the air
I surrender all to You
Lord,
At least let me have faith of a mustard seed
Believing You will do the incredible

Lord,
I pray for the spirit of trust to enter my body
Relying on You and not my own understanding
Let me feel safe in the midst of chaos

I had to get off my high horse
So I am landing
Next to you
I am standing

Solid as a rock that You are,
I am coming closer Lord
Drawing near
Not far

I thank you in advance
For the things to come,
I pray to keep my hands in your hands
In Jesus name,
Amen.

But God

My child,
"I will never leave you nor forsake you,
I sit high and look low,
No weapon formed against you shall prosper,
Do you know who I am?
I am the Alpha and the Omega,
The beginning and the end,
The first and the last,
I Am King,
The one and only King with a train that fills the temple,
The same King who designed your cheeks with dimples,
You lack understanding
I'm deeper than simple
Your eyes will never see all of My potential
You're not as intelligent as you think,
You wouldn't be able to calculate the width of My figure,
The capacity of My weight
Even if you tried
I am too big for your mind to think
Just trust Me and follow
No need to worry
Suck it up
But then again
I am too big for your throat to swallow"

But God,
Why do I feel alone?
You said You would never leave me, nor forsake me
But God,
Here I am on my own
I feel invisible
Standing clearly here
I feel You pass me by without contact
I guess I am just not there
Are You looking in my direction,
As You sit high and look low?
All I feel is devastation
Weapons formed like robbery
I am under attack
Drowning in my own sweat
Why do You let me suffer?
What happened to You
Being the Alpha and the Omega,
The beginning and the end,
The first and the last,
The King?

"My child,
You have yet to comprehend who I Am
Do you hear yourself?
You don't get because you don't give
You are selfish

All about how you feel
You feel alone because you refuse to let Me in
I never left you
Even when you turned your back
Questioning who I Am
I Am always right there
Yes!
I Am everything I say I Am
Don't fault me for your lack of understanding,
Blame yourself
You have allowed the toxicity of the world to suck you in
Polluting your mind with garbage
Yet, I wait for you to draw near to me
I want to be close
Side by side"
Lately all I hear from you is, "But God"

Father,
I am sorry,
I am lost and confused
Father, I repent to You
Let me turn from my ways
And face Your ways
Lord, fill me with the spirit of Abraham,
Faithful and obedient
Fill me with the spirit of Moses,
Meek and humble

Fill me with the spirit of Daniel,
Courageous
Fill me with the spirit of Job,
Righteous
Fill me up God
For I am empty
But God,
I know you can make me full
Lay out my path that I may walk upon
God,
Bless my journey ahead
In Jesus name,
Amen.

God so Loved...

John 3:16
God so loved the world
He gave His only Son
Whoever believes will not perish
They will have eternal life
God made a sacrifice
Gave His Son,
His only One

Father, what You did
Exceeds anything I could ever do
I look up to You
Admire Your power
You are powerful

What You did,
You did not have to
You love hard
We should love hard too
You do not give up on us
We should not give up on you

Father,
Guide our feet
Let us walk in our purpose

Let us step in place
Getting in formation to reach our destiny

I love You
You love me
You are the truth
All the glory belongs to You

Fill Me Up

I am empty
Nothing left to give to society
I am incomplete
Do not know how much longer I have to live
But bring the match,
I want to be on fire for You
Turning pages of the Bible
Speaking tongues with your words
I want to know all about You

Let me open up
Allowing You to inject me with Your spirit
Use me
Let the world see You through me
Fill me up God

I am a cleaned up sinner
Ready to march in Your kingdom
My feet are dusted off
My skin has been removed
My soul has been replaced
You gave me a new mood
Fill me up God

I am hungry
Looking at the menu
Only thing that looks appetizing is You
So I order the Holy Ghost combo
With a side of praise
Blessings are dollar bills
You make it rain
Fill me up God

Whatever You have
I will take
Send the blessings my way
I will share with my neighbor
You said it's better to give than receive anyway
Fill me up God

Lift my spirit to the heavens
Yes, I sinned and repented
That's my confession
I want a personality like Jesus
Ready to sacrifice all
I am down for the cause
Fill me up God

Fill me with an abundance of love
Fill me with rainbows and butterflies
Fill me with breeze and sunshine
Fill me up God

I am ready to live
Too afraid to die
Make me full with filling
Fill me up God

Love Me

A teaspoon of
A cup
A tablespoon of
A quart
I want Your love in larger measurements
Every day my portion goes up

I follow the recipe of Your heart
A gallon of love that's bubbling over
With the same amount of
Faith, hope, and trust

Mmmm,
I need more and more of You
I cannot sleep
I cannot eat
Desperate
Going crazy
Whenever we are apart

Overdose me
With love
Knock me out
With blessings
Put me to sleep
With Your touch

Hold me gently, Lord
I need Your protection
Comfort me
Love does no harm to the body
So love me

Love is not rushed
Be patient
Love is not malicious
Be pleasant
You, God is Love

Let me sow love
So I can reap
Be with me,
That I may love
The way You love me

Beauty For Ashes

Where there is death,
There is life
God takes
Beauty for ashes
Turning mourning to joy
Taking me from dirt
And designed me as an art piece

Now I am worth being on the walls of Museums
Showcase the beauty for ashes
Rather than being
Dark and gray
Smoky
Burning from the heat of negativity

The beauty of it all
God can make any bad situation
And structure it to something positive
Hope is the key
When ashes fall in your life

Marriages may be messed up
Kids not acting right
Jobs are a headache
But you go anyway to make a piece of change
Hope

Things will get better
Shoulders were not meant to stay cold
Tears never stay wet
Eventually they dry up
God fixes broken hearts that have been cracked

Gives sun to the cloudy sky
Gives peace to dysfunctional
Gives the opportunity to life
To everything that has potential to die
He gives beauty for ashes

I am a cut diamond
Shaping the form of a crown
To beam the light of a perfect sparkle
Lord you gave me quality
Even in my iniquity

I was an angry soul
Held grudges bigger than I
Hated every man that I laid eyes on
Could not rest
Twisting and turning
Eyes rolling
Exhausted just from the sight of them walking away
Without looking back
To see if I was ok

So I put a chain lock on my heart
It was hard for me to love
I thought I was so smart
Figuring out every way
To dodge the bullets
To a broken heart
I was sharp
Until my brain caught a fart

I was running out of options
And from there I ran into You
You see the beauty inside of my ashes
I am rich with Your blessings
I am living lavish

But I come to You in my bumpy road
Asking You to pave the way
Smooth me out
Continue to craft me
With the palms of Your in-depth hands
Mold me to Your liking
Give me beauty for ashes

My mind tends to go to waste
But there You catch it
Before it is too late
My thoughts You paste
So it will not be all over the place

You gave me sense of direction
Directing me to the center stage
Letting my presence fill the room
And my voice reach every cochlear
To tell the world about You
It is not about being popular

I just want my ashes to be beautified
You blew out my matches
Covered up my patches
Oh Savior of my crashes
You gave me beauty for ashes

Starts with U – N - I

It starts with U-N-I
So spill the T
Y?
Because it must begin somewhere
If we want to come together as one
U-N-I need to initiate
Bringing people to the Son

Church is missing unity
Separated by personal desires
No one can agree
It is not about being one anymore
We are all about me

Who made us King?
Ruling the world
We all want to be a boss
When did we ever die for another?
Made a sacrifice on the cross

Our ego is way too high
We need to cut it
Pretending to be something we are not
Why do we be frontin'?
Father,
Bring unity into our hearts

Remove self from the goal that we are trying to reach
Our minds, Father
Set it free

It all starts with U-N-I
So spill the T
Y?
Because it must begin somewhere
If we want to come together as one
U-N-I need to initiate
Bringing people to the Son

With U-N-I
We can accomplish anything
It may seem hard now
But it will feel worth it at the end
To know,
The battle we have won

All Souls Matter

Skin is rich
Deeper than you and I
But the mind should be even richer
Than us combined

The mind is larger than skin
So, why blame skin on the shooting?
When really it is the man's mind

Skin do not kill,
It is sin
Traumatic minds
Wicked thoughts creeping in

My heart bleeds
Love has been taken away
From our minds
We have been brain washed
Military style
Trained to kill
Our enemies
Nobody turns the other cheek
To some that sounds ridiculous

My Lord,
I can only imagine
How you are feeling
To know
Your children are murderers
Killing the vibe that you initiated
Now everything's chaotic
Yet, we want to sugar coat
Running from the truth
So we abbreviate it

We are so stuck on
The battle of
"Black lives matter"
And
"All lives matter"
But what about the souls?

Our focus point should be on
How many souls we can save
Before these lives are taken away
Because that is what matters

We all have to die anyway
But are we all going to live?
Or, are we going to continue to fall in the arms of the Devil?
Weakness is all He gives

Father,
Take the veils from over our eyes
So we can see the trap we are tangled in
Drum our head
Bring rhythm to our feet
Help us to stay on beat
Our heart is becoming fallen music

We need you more than ever
The world is spinning in the opposite direction
Quickly
I am feeling a little woozy
I am getting dizzy
Vomiting from disgust
Society is not up
They all are sleeping
When are we going to wake up?
It is almost evening

Earthly Dad

Earthly dad,
This Father's Day
I gave you the gift of forgiveness
Asked God to remove the pain and hurt from my being

It wasn't for you
Forgiveness is for self
My soul was rudely awakened
But the Lord put it to rest

Yes,
I sought for your attention and time
Seemed like I kept coming at the last minute
Nothing was left for me
You always ran out of time

I was tired of being hurt
Tired of letting anger consume all of my energy
Holding me back from getting hurt by others
It was my security

It was already enough being destroyed by you
I just could not take any more
I could not get near to people
I felt like it was dangerous

Could not get too close to anyone
I felt like it was contagious
So I always washed my hands
Being done before anything got started

Was not trying to make relationships
Fear of commitment
So I would rather not put myself in that state
Of mind
Your own business
Was more important

I started acting ugly towards you
Until it ate my conscience
I felt uninvited
Fatherless
Living in a house
Feeling so homeless

But Dad
I am over it now
Was not easy
But I never stop praying to God
I did not know how to trust
You never showed me how

Lord forgive him
For he knows not what he does
Let him start today
Being a better father
For not just his kids
But his grandchildren too
In Jesus name,
Amen.

I'm Intoxicated

Poisoned with a love potion
Mixed with a spice of.....
I wish I never did it
Sober until becoming wasted
Stumbling, standing still
Going out of my mind
Battling about how I feel

Throwing up everything I can remember
Hang over your head
Things you have done
Last January through December

Memory became my best friend
Keeping me updated of the suspicion
I see rejection getting near
So close I can feel
As if it was intimate

I am intoxicated
So drunk
That my mind is unconscious
Sometimes I lose it
Until I am clueless
Of what I have done and am doing

Anger is toxic
Has me discombobulated
Where I withdraw from focus
My mind was once taken over
By some ungodly spirits
That were trying to kill me
I had one too many

One day I took my last shot
I wanted love without the poison
Love sometimes can become dangerous
But caution, we start avoiding

Crazy love isn't really that sexy
I never saw the lingerie
All I saw was a dressed-up truth
That never became naked
Lies you tell
Phrases are cliché
Lies are not even white
It was more like ivory

But I walked away from the story
I never imagined reading
Sometimes we pick up the wrong book
But never want to close it
Because the mind is intrigued by curiosity

The unknown is exciting
But we must be careful
Where we look for security

No one can protect like God
So keep your mind on Him
If you are looking to be amazed
He is ready to surprise
He has so much up his sleeve
That we cannot even see with our own eyes

Father,
From now on,
Where you lay
Is where I lie
I will walk on the path that you laid out
I will not be clumsy,
Tripping over what you have asked of me
I will just try
I will reach your people
With the words you drew
Out in my heart
Showing off the art
You have designed
I will wear it like it is the latest fashion
You gave me a neat crease
Without using an iron

Putting me together so perfectly
You fold me
Tucked the old version of me away
Father,
Continue to make me new
In Jesus name,
Amen.

Trapped

It's hard to see the light
When you're blinded,
It's hard to stay focused
When you're surrounded
By temptation

Have you ever been trapped by your own desires?
Can't escape lust
When bodies are exhibited
Streets are now museums
Showing off the art of raunchiness
A sick but creative freedom of uniqueness

Females are stuck in a state of
Self-disrespect
Being careless
Constantly losing moral
Fabric, they treat like you, and reject

Less is more
The story is deeper than the skimpy clothes

Portraying stacks of confidence
When actually they have none at all
Doing everything within their means
To get a guy to turn his head in their direction
Sending the wrong impression

Have you ever been trapped by your thirst?
Thirsty for alcohol
Dehydrated in fact
Bars become sanctuaries
A place where alcoholics worship
Bartenders are their gods
Creating broken-heeled models
Passing drinks until they get wasted
Nicely decorated
Sin wrapped in a bottle

Have you ever been trapped?
Addicted to the nicotine
Every time you look around
Two fingers to the mouth
Inhaling peace
The sign that is

Lungs are dying
Yes it's the truth
But when you're so accustomed to old habits
It's hard to stop
And start something new

Have you ever been trapped in abuse?
Can't walk away
So you stay
Believing that he loves you
Your mind is trained to think
That it was you
As you look at the scars and bruises
You convince yourself
It's your fault
Lord knows it's not true

It's time to walk away
Let go and let God
Lean not on your own understanding
Get in position to follow
He's ready to guide

Take it to Your Sister

Sisters in Christ
Why are we not getting along?
What is up with the sisterhood?
Where did we take a left turn, and go wrong?
We should have each other's back
Not to put a knife in it
Twisting and turning
Going deeper to kill them

If you have a problem
Why not go to that sister?
Give her a chance to live
Instead of running around the church
Slandering her name
Complaining about what she is doing
But what makes you any better
When you are doing the same

My sisters,
Why bash the work of others?
At least they stepped up and tried to do something
See,
The main ones who have their mouths open
Are the same ones who are not doing anything
Sound like someone needs to shut up
And stop judging

Who made them God?
What cross did they die on?
Please someone tell me
I need to know
The Bible says to judge not
Let us put a period
That is the small dot
At the end of a sentence
Telling us to stop

My sisters,
Why are we not getting along?
What is up with the sisterhood?
Where did we take a left turn, and go wrong?

Gossip,
We sure are good at
Fighting over a man
That is not ours
Really,
What are we doing?

Older sisters,
What are you showing the younger ones?
Can they rely on you for proper growth?
Or has the milk been in the breast for too long?
Spoiled
But yet you still serving left overs

It is time for us to do something
Taking us out of the equation
It is not about me
And it sure ain't about you
There is someone greater

My sisters,
If you have an issue with your sister
Take it to her like a woman
Do not go behind her back talking crap
That is what little girls do
Do not be a devilish child
But a Christian woman, who can handle her own

"Father,
I ask that you be with the sisterhood
Let us stop hating on the next
Let us stop gossiping, slandering, and all other malicious acts."

"Father,
Why are we not getting along?
What is up with the sisterhood?
Where did we take a left turn and go wrong?"

Healing

Jeremiah 17:14

Heal me, Lord, and I will be healed; save me Lord and I will be saved, for you are the one I praise.

Some are wounded and broken
Hungry and thirsty
Homeless and lost
Weak
Heal them Lord
Save them from all of calamity

Give strength to those who been weakened
Then they will be strong,
Give faith to the doubtful
So they can believe
Turn them away from their wrongs

Husbands and wives are fighting
The relationship
They cannot manage
You are God, who can salvage
Any disconnected marriage

Heal the sick
Shelter the poor

Hold on to the sinners
For they need you more

Slaughter the vindictive malevolent ways of man
So they will not cause any harm out of revenge
Besides,
What does being malicious solve?
When you will have to pay for it at the end

Heal us Lord
And we will be healed
Save us Lord
And we will be saved
For you are the one we praise

Let us remember 17:14 in the book or Jeremiah
Let us be faithful and trust you like Hezekiah
Let us set goals
And succeed in all our endeavors
All you give
Let us treasure

Pray,
"No matter how hard things seem
God can always make it better
Be aware,
Your trust in the Lord, Rewarded with answered prayers"

Living in Silence

Silent
She kept quiet
Scared to make a move
Embarrassed
From the hit
That marked the bruise

Living in a hard place
Voices are loud in her head
But she tunes it out
Continues to be engaged
To that abusive man who made her black out

She makes it all look good
With her pretend smile
And make-up that covers her body
To hide the loneliness,
The sadness and depression,
To hide the fright
She does not want to show any signs of weakness
Wishes it all will end
Just as fast as it started

Silence was the cover-up
Hiding her emotions in a cosmetic bag

Far too long
It is time to unzip it
Pulling out all of her beauty products
That God had originally purchased

Her smile should have never turned into an act
I am praying to God
That the Devil can be nice enough for a change
And hand her joy back
He was that thief who stole it

Mirrors
She hated
Giving her a reflection of a person
God never created

She became haunted
By her own clone that was daunted,
Messed with her mind
Turned her away from God
Now, he is "Most Wanted"
Silent
She kept quiet
Scared to make a move
Embarrassed
From the hit
That marked the bruise

Living in a hard place
Voices are loud in her head
But she tunes it out
Continues to be engaged
To that abusive man who made her black out

Until one day,
God took over
Brought her to a dramatic storm
Letting her life flash right before her eyes
Trying to get her to wake up
To see
That man will eventually cause her to die
And that HE is the only one who can save her

God opens the door,
But is she ready to ride?
She's a turtle
Moving slow
With a hard shell
That is used for shelter
It was her go-to place
When she was scared to look people in their face
Afraid they will see right through her

Every day she drinks tears for water
Thirsty for the pain to go away

She was alone and unhappy
Naturally, she isolated herself from her family

She was living in silence
It was the most painful
Living without life
Becomes unknowingly dangerous

Sometimes we must die to live
Taking all the bullets out of the gun
Empty she has become
Now there is room for the Son to enter

She began with a prayer
That says,
Lord let me be
Faithful and obedient

Take away my baggage
Clean me up so I can be worthy
To step foot in your kingdom

Give me a new home
Revise my life
Give me a better one
You never gave up on me
Not once or twice

My heart I ask for purification
From the variation of heartache and devastation
Give me a heart of forgiveness
Especially for that abusive man
That caused me to black out
Had me living in a hard place
With voices loud in my head that I tuned out
Lord forgive him
In Jesus name,

That was her prayer
For so long
She was living in silence
She kept quiet
Scared to make a move
Embarrassed
From the hit
That marked the bruise

Living in a hard place
Voices are loud in her head
But she tunes it out
Continues to engage
With that abusive man who made her black out

But she says,
NO MORE!!!

Put her trust and strength in God
She realized, she is royal
Once she found her gold

She and God switched roles
Now,
He's the driver in her car
She can relax
Leaning back
Letting God be in full control

I'm That You

Broken heart
Broken truth
Broken trust
Broken you
Fell into pieces

Sweep
Broom with no dust pan
Everything's piling up
Giving it to you God
You can pick it all up

Trials and tribulations are mine
I own them
An important piece of the puzzle
Tucked under the sheet
Can't get rid of
When problems are left incomplete

Broken heart
Broken truth
Broken trust
Broken you
Fell into pieces

Father,
I'm that "you" who fell
Broken from all of the lies and disappointment
All the pieces were there
But I steadily try to find what was missing
It was you, Lord
That person I needed

You know me inside out
You designed me with emotions
You're the only one who can figure them out

My heart was broken
From all the lies
Which caused me not to trust
It was hard to get close to people
I never could gain an "us"

Broken heart
Broken truth
Broken trust
Broken you
No, broken me
I was that "you"
Who fell into pieces
Completely

Put a Period

Chains I break
A prisoner
I ain't
No more
I broke the bars to the gate
Walked straight out on faith
I put a period to my sentence
A prisoner
I ain't

Life is a sentence
I have to complete
I am given two options
Do right and be free
Or continue to look to Hell for eternity

Summer is overrated
So I know I cannot spend a minute in hell
I cannot be blazed
The heat I cannot take
Officers,
Where is the key?
Open this cell
I cannot spend life in this jail

The world is trying to hold me down
Nailing my feet to the ground
Inserting false beliefs to my mind
But my brain rejects it
Jesus gives me hope
Nothing can stop me now

Chains I break
A prisoner
I ain't
No more
I broke the bars to the gate
Walked straight out on faith
I put a period to my sentence
A prisoner
I ain't

Hands will not be cuffed
They are free to touch
Lives that are lost,
Mixed in the sinful stuff

Heaven dreamed
Soon will be reality
Flying away from Earth
To get to destiny

My purpose I seek
God gives opportunity
And I am going to take it
Quite aware of the price
Nothing comes for free
I will pay it
It is what it is
I cannot shake it

Father,
I am thankful for your thanksgiving
Grateful for your grace
Ecstatic for your ecstasy
All the joy you bring

Chains were over me
I have been charged
With a long sentence
But it is void

Time would have been myriad
Prison was not for me
So I put a period
Was not going to let anything stop my growth
I am no idiot

Chains I break

A prisoner

I ain't

No more

I broke the bars to the gate

Walked straight out on faith

I put a period to my sentence

A prisoner

I ain't

Surrender

I hear the sirens,
Your voice beating in my head
Lord you are calling,
I did not immediately answer
I ignored you instead

I hear the sirens
Capturing my attention,
I begin to run
Thought I could get away,
That was my intention

I hear the sirens
Loud and deep
My ears start opening
My eyes seek
Looking for where the noise was coming from

Right where I was standing
I saw your presence for once
Hands up,
Do not shoot me down
I surrender my all to you God

I give up
I give in
First things seemed odd
Now, it looks even

I threw my hands in the air
Said, no more!
I cannot do it all by myself
I need you Lord

I am sorry
I brushed You off far too long
You warned me about this old world
I was a fool,
Just did not listen

I was aware
I would be tempted
Without your armor
There is not any protection

I was weak,
Letting the Devil devour me
I had no strength
I needed your power indeed
I surrender

Do away with this flesh of mine
Let me live in your spirit
Aware of my limits
I reject anything you prohibit
Let me live in your image

The world I threw from my mind
I am opening up so you can enter
I am giving it all to you God
I surrender

Right on Time

I hear the cries of your children, Father
Silent yet loud
Needing you right now
In the name of Jesus
Your grace cannot be without

Their past unconsciously haunts them
They are trying to move forward
Somehow the rear is always behind
Causing their minds to be guarded

What they thought was first
Let it now seem last
Rearrange their minds
Until they can no longer recognize their past

We need your strength, Father
To be a better individual
It is hard to face this world alone
I know you are there
We cannot do anything on our own

For Your Word says,
"Ask and it will be given,
Seek and you shall find,
Knock and the door will open"
Lord you show up right on time

Shadows of Death

Mirrors I walk on
Distinctive reflections
Images of my journey
Shadows of death
Far from your protection

Every step away from you
I am slowly dying
You design me as a flower
Beauty that blossoms
Instead, I am a black rose
Steadily dying

Have nothing in common
With the original blueprint
My soul is different
The world got involved
Evolving me to its liking

I been entangled
Wrapped tightly
Walked miles
Hurting feet
Soul burning
Exhausted spirit

Lord please teach
I am in a position for learning

I been trapped in a circle
Going round and round
But far as I can see
There is no escape
All around is fire
Scared to feel it
But it was me
Volunteered for the center

I thought in order to get in
It was required for me to be able to fit in
Lord, I was wrong
Asking for your forgiveness
For my spirit is in constant battle with flesh
Spirit weakened

Lord, I ask that you remove the shadows
Hand me a light bulb
Replace the lost electricity
Electrolyze my being
I want to die in you
You are to die for
Delight me with your light, Lord

Shine down on me
Enter this old vessel of mine
Let me walk with reflections of you in me
I need the Son to beam
Staining the ground with your shadow
That surrounds me

Lord,
I am all yours now
I pray I never revisit the shadows of death
Walking on mirrors
With distinctive reflections,
Images of my journey that I regret
I realize I need you to protect

Lord,
Please do not give up on me
I am ready to follow your command
Raise this black rose into that beautiful flower
I am ready to blossom
In Jesus name,
Amen.

Found in the Pages

Lost but was found in the pages of my notebook
Things around me were falling apart
I thought I was all alone
Until I saw Your hand reached out
There were You God helping me up

See,
I fall
But I did not fail,
Failure is quitting
So I never give up
I dust myself off
Because I got to get somewhere

I have been hurt
But I will not be destroyed
I have been misconstrued
But I will not let it define me
Misconception I withdrew

Every mistake
Takes me through
Wisdom 101
Teaching me about life
And how to trigger the gun

Shooting down a piece of me
That does not deserve to be just tapped with a knife

I could not sugar coat the truth
I was not sweet enough to even want to
My smile was a mask
To cover-up the Devil,
My veins were not always flowing with the blood of Jesus
It was liquid that has formed into metal
Somehow I invited the world in
It took my royalty and made it devalued

But God,
You gave me Your Son
Jesus was my rescue
Showing up just in time
Saving me from the mistakes that I was close to showing my nephew
My old ways became blocked from my lil' man's view
If only he saw the preview

Thank you God
For giving me sense to fix the path in which I promenade
The better my steps,
Then, your ways
I can properly demonstrate

I was lost but was found in the pages of my notebook

Writing down the pain
And things I overcame,
You gave me a gift
So I will shower others with it
As if I was making it rain

Transformation

Out in the world
Lost but kept finding things to get into
Out in the world
Danger I ran into

Broken but attached to misery
It loved company
It was the only attention given
Soaked in despair
Convenient
I bathe in betrayal

World turned upside down
Nothing seemed fair
To fix the hurt
I had to start somewhere
So I began with prayer

Hate was loved deeply
The only consistency in life
Love was sometimey
I smoothly sought anger
I was looking for stability

Unsolved problems,
Life is filled with complicated equations
That are difficult to solve
There was always the unknown
For so long
I tried to figure out that x

The missing variable was always there
I feel like an ignorant genius
Eyes begin to open to the solution
Now I can see You Jesus

I give my life to You
Including my problems
You can solve them better than I can
You are an undeniable spirit
And I am just a fleshly man

I began
To give you a chance
Instantly, I saw the transformation
A sprit inside of me
Polished like new
You gave me confirmation
No more denying You

I saw the demons
Knocking on the door
Politeness and curiosity let them in
They wanted my soul
In exchange,
I got the privilege to taste them
Leaving a bad taste in my mouth
Filled with filth

Lips vomit out with hurting vocabulary
Made up words
I became an author of my own dictionary
Reading it out loud to be heard

I pray to you Father
To change me now
Giving me eyes of your wants from me
So I can give it times three

You are the only one I want to worship
Continue to transform me into your liking
Transition me from the world to your Kingdom
Lord, supply me with Your wisdom

Remodel

Thank you for deliverance
Thank you for allowing me
To be strong in You to forgive him

Yes, he was the cause of all my pain
Yes, I wanted things to change
Yes, I wish he taught me about a man
Yes, I wish he was there to comfort me when I was sad
Even though he did not,
I still should not have acted ugly towards my dad
So my bad

I was bleeding inside
Not the way I should have been though
Over flowed with hurt
The enemy was killing me slow
Understand now
When my mama use to say,
"Misery loves company"
So
I am older now
I am riding solo

I only weigh 120 pounds
Burdens are heavy

It is easy to get pulled down
But harder to get back up
The closer I get to you
The more he is in my ear with temptation
But I tell him to shut up

Fed up
Over it
Been mad too long
He is a thief in the night
I give him a taste of his own medicine
Taking back joy that I once owned

Christ-I-am
Not exactly
But if you knock one hump off the m
You will see
I am a Christ-i-an
Yes, a Christian

Lord you gave me a new attitude
Laid out the runway
I am ready to work it
Displaying my smile
My lips are a model
My teeth you will see for a while
Lord you made me new

Here I come again
I think they call that
A remodel

Worship With No Regret

What you have for me God
Let me receive it
What you want from me God
Let me give it

My knees are meeting what is underneath me
My hands finally met
My head bowed
Eyes closed
I worship you with no regret

I love you
You first loved me
It took some time to recognize
Sometimes what is in front of us,
We just do not see

I do not want to be blinded any more
You already showed Yourself to me
No need to show any more
I believe everything You are
And all You have in store

So long I suffered with anger
Now I am quick to listen, slow to speak, and slow to get angry

You are my insurance
I come to You in my accidents
It was You who gave me deliverance

I am delivered
Not the person I was yesterday
Today, I am someone different
I became naked
Taking off everything that was insignificant
Clothes were my weakness
I purchased a new wardrobe
Now I am rocking Jesus

What You have for me God
Let me receive it
What You want from me God
Let me give it
My knees are meeting what is underneath me
My hands finally met
My head bowed
Eyes closed
I worship you with no regret

This is How I Sleep

This is how I sleep
Well,
Before Chris came
This is how I use to sleep
Before Chris and my kid's father

Cannot believe
Hmmm...
I traded in my God for a man
My God?
Hmm...
What was I thinking?

I knew he could never replace You
But I was just enjoying the moment
My time was tied up
So tight
I could not even squeeze You in
Like I used to do
Feeling like I am treating You as the opponent

You could have gone into defense mood
And fouled me out
Both times
You did not

When I tell you,
Man,
I got something to shout about
I hope you listeners, are listening

Yes,
I was faithful at first
Studying Your Word to get close
But here comes a raggedy "man"
OK....
A grown boy
Turning me away
Can I blame him?
No
Wish I could
But I can't

It was me
Falling short of the glory of God
I am not perfect
We all have things to tweak
I am just sorry
I allowed my flesh
To fall so weak

I was a solider in my own army
My spirit took an about-face from You

Marching to my own commands
Going at my own pace

Well, well, well
Look where it got me
I learned my lesson now
All eyes on me
Feeling slight judge-y

One turned to two
I was clumsy
Falling for the same guy
Both was worldly

Now I am looking for a man of God
To hold me down in Your Word
Life was becoming a playground
Where I dropped the ball
Recess is over
I heard the ring of the alarm
Let me run
Right back into Your arms

After my kid's father
There was Chris
I checked out
He was cheap

Did not pay the price
Instead of putting a period to the end of his name
I inserted a t
Coming up with Christ
That is who I am back rolling with
See life is nice

I picked up my books again
No more of kid's father
No more Chris
I dropped the two of them

See,
Now I am looking for my husband
That you have designed for me
I was a backslidden Christian,
Who came back better than before
You never gave up on me
Books are back on the bed to study
Rather than on the floor
More of You I seek
From now on,
This is how I sleep

Story behind "This Is How I Sleep"

This Is How I Sleep was given life about a woman of God I met on my journey. While single, she lost her way and backslid due to love encounters with two different men. God once was her pride and joy. She confessed that after she put down her study books, her mind became entangled with conflict between God and man. She almost put them on the same level.

Her conscience ate away at her as time proceeded on. She prayed day after day and night after night, that God would deliver her and eliminate sin from her life. Finally, she walked away from man and began walking with God again. Now she is back on fire for God and waiting patiently for Him to send her a husband fit for her.

Her inspiring story needed to be told because so many times a woman's hunger and thirst for a man compels her to accept anyone. Even if God did not send him.

From her tests, we find this testimony - - God never leaves or forsakes you. He saves you from all sin. Never stop believing and praying.

I give to others the same testimony!

Never

Stop

Praying

POEMS

Many Questions

I been thinking for some time now
Of the Day of Judgment
How will my review go?
I have so many questions

Answers only the Lord knows
Patient but impatient to hear the response
It's life or death
Did I react in my flesh or rely on my soul?
I hope eternity awaits me

Was I faithful unto thee?
Did I live my life to the fullest?
While remembering to act like a Christian
Did I do what I was made to do?
Did I figure out my destiny or allow it to pass me by?

Did I become blind and didn't seek You enough?
Was I patient or always in a rush?
I know I am fast-paced
Doing so much in one day
But did I take out enough time to get to know You better?
Or did I treat You like a misspelled word in a letter and scratch You out?
Realize I cannot take away You

You are un-edited
But me on the other hand
I can draw a line through
Remove the bad and make new
But have I done that for You
Was I true?

Did I lust over the things of the world,
or break my neck just to follow You?
Would You reply back yes?
Letting me know I am not perfect
And yes, I reacted in my flesh
Did things I should not have done
Said things I should not have said
But on the other hand
I remembered You during the process
I changed my ways
Was it too late?

Everything, I will have to get account of
Life is a credit card that gets abused,
Swiped for fun
But at the end there is a statement
Showing how much damage has been done

Give In

Don't give up
Give in
Repent
Turn away from sin
God is in control
So to Him
Give in

Let go of your problems
God will slowly expose the purpose
The blessing is inside the mystery
So let go

Do not give up
Sometimes challenges come and they go
God knows all about it
To Him
Bow down
Yourself
You submit

Let go
Of the pain
Things could be worse
Nothing was made to work

The way man imagines it to
So let go

Times get hard
Water turns into ice
Shapes form
In order to break the ice
(Joke, Laugh hard)

Cannot be too serious
Joy may pass right by
Within a glimpse of an eye
Keep site of what is ahead
Never look back
Look high
There is the prize
Above the sky

Do not give up
Give in
Everything else has failed
So try Jesus
There is no greater Friend

Stop trying to do everything by yourself
Give the situation to Him
Do not give up
Just give in

Run to God

Do not run from
Run to
God is waiting on you
Run

He should not have to track you down
Life is similar to a race
Trying to beat your opponent
Who is on the other side
But God is with you
Right in your face
Run to
Do not hide

I know it is hard right now
Finances are few
Bills are overdue
Everyone has their hand out for their money
You just don't know what to do
Run to

Some are sick in their hospital bed
Need a tube to get fed
Cannot get up

But just pray to God
I promise He will show up

I see my grandma's
Meds are maxed out
Suffering with different medical issues
Like arthritis, a weak heart and I think gout
But don't give up
Run

This battle is not yours
What are you standing there for?
Go give it to the Lord
He got you
You just have to
Run to

Jobs are stressful
Dealing with people is not always pleasant
It is hard to see the different views
So many mixed personalities
Like lighting a fuse

School may be getting hard
Teachers are not teaching like they used to
Cafeterias are serving upsetting portions
Students' minds are empty

While their feet are rocking Jordans
What is going on?
What is really the importance?

Marriages are not always working
Husbands and wives are fighting
Both are failing to give one hundred
But hold on
Divorce should not be an option

It takes two with the help of God to be strong
In this thing called marriage
Every wound deserves a bandage
You may be confused
Wondering where the drama has begun
It is not easy
Do not be quickly done

Do not run from
Run to
God is waiting on you
So run

One Man's Journey, Another Man's Lifestyle

Man's lifestyle
Reflects from the man's journey,
Striving to be like Him
Who is the author of our life story
Whose book has been the #1 best seller since before time

It was Him,
Walking bare footed
Leaving His foot prints
Hoping we would follow the path of righteousness
Instead of running from the feet that gave us a mouth to eat
Ears to hear
Feelings to feel

He is the real big foot
That people seek
But no one sees
Knowing he is still there

Having faith
Believing what we cannot see
Trying to figure this world out
As if it is a maze

One man's journey
Becomes another man's lifestyle

Learning from the different stages of life
Styling to perfection
Making a good impression
Walking by faith and not by sight

See, it was His journey that got us here
It was His journey that led Him into being crucified
Just for us to live again
But some choose to die
Cannot look past the sky
After all he has done
Some will not even have the courtesy to breathe beyond the Earth
As if they were blinded by the Son

One man's journey
Becomes another man's lifestyle
Working to receive a check,
A check with figures that are unthought-of
Nothing can amount to,
You get what you work for
Not work just to get everything taken from you
And have a little left over
Just to get by

It was His journey that caused us to be inspired from His inspiration

Letting us know that sometimes we will be tempted with temptation

We will have trials and tribulations

And at those times

We must stay strong

And not break from the roots

Letting go of his feet

When we have no more food to eat

Act like we only can praise Him

When we have everything we want and need

His journey should be our lifestyle

Somehow,

We get so wrapped up in the worldly things

When it comes to giving the Lord Jesus all the glory and praise

We cannot improvise

We began to be so selfish

Focusing only on what "I need" or "I want"

The world spoils us with the things we want

Turning it into an addiction

We can have all the things we want on Earth

As well as in Heaven

As long as we take heed to the words of the Bible

Just listen

But sometimes we are deaf

Ears can no longer hear the sound waves of His voice
We invite the world into our ears
Now it's stuffed
So much have been falsified
Wondering where we go from here

Searching in the classified section of our newspaper
Wondering which story to buy
Sometimes we pick up the wrong book
To tell us about our lifetime
If you were smart like me
You will pick up that B.I.B.L.E
To get you through life
The good and the down times
Everything you need is there
Evidence
That his journey should be your lifestyle
He is who you live by
Residents

He will save you
Once you hear the gospel, believe, repent, confess, and be baptized
Go down, old man
Come up new
God had this plan way back when
And it still stands for you

Chains are Broken

Chains are broken
Heart is now open
Open to love
Something you taught me
Better yet, showed me
Once you entered my world

Dreams came to life
The day I imagined
You as my husband
And I as your wife
For better or worst
Til death do us part

My lungs are becoming your lungs
My breath is your breath
My space is your space
We breathe at the same time,
At the same pace

I place my ear against your chest
Instantly,
I hear the rhythm of your heartbeat
Beating exactly like mine
I continue to listen

Lying next to you
In tune with the sound

It sounded like music
Spiritual words
So I continue to listen
Focusing on the words as if it was the Bible
And I was the perfect Christian

I love you
For a multitude of reasons
I love you
Love the way you love me
And accept me for who I am
Looking not past my flaws
But directly at them
And you still love me deeply

Your love is equivalent
To the love Jesus has for the church
You have that Jesus love
Putting swag on everything
You have taste
S.W.A.G.
Saved **W**ith **A**mazing **G**race

Tying the knot
Does not mean

It is a noose around your neck
Leaving you choking
But it is a powerful force
Around the two of you
Bonding and exploring
The beauty of love

Marriage is a beautiful thing
A job where you must be qualified
To listen, communicate, sacrifice, and never give up
No matter how hard it gets
A job where you sign up to be there around the clock,
This job is permanent

Days do not always have sunshine
Sometimes it is cloudy
Pouring rain outside
But God is in control
If you put Him first
Everything will work

From your ribs,
I saw birth
But don't get it twisted,
It was my Creator who made me
Yes, you love me
But see, He loved me first

We may not have everything we want
But the Bible tells us to be content
God said,
"Never will I leave you,
Nor will I forsake you"
So put your trust in Him
Cannot always go to friends
Sometimes you must go to Him to vent

"He who finds a wife,
Finds a good thing and obtains favor from the Lord
A wife of noble character is her husband's crown
But a disgraceful wife is like decay in his bones"
Wife, submit to your husband
Husband, love your wife
Never let her feel alone

On the wedding day,
I can hear the preacher say,
"From this day forward,
I pronounce you husband and wife"
Partners in crime
No,
Partners in Christ

Wife to your husband submit
Husband, love your wife

Even as Christ loves the church
For He gave His life for it

Chains are broken
Heart is now open
Open to love
Something you taught me
Better yet showed me
Once you entered my world

Loved One, Lost One

Tears of water
Falling in the deep
Discombobulated
Mouth unable to speak

Numb
Up
But dreaming
How could this be?
Loved one, lost one
It seems too soon for me

Hearts of broken glass
Minds of scrambled eggs
So emotional
Bring breakfast to bed

Cannot get up
Really do not want to
Knees are grills
Burning from being on them
Asking, why Lord?

Eyes are glued open
Cannot blink

Even if I wanted to
Body is in shock
To die; is supposed to

Cannot believe
It was just yesterday
Was laughing on the phone
Today the answer was different
A call to go home

Daddy called
Time to go
Some things have no control
But yet a reason
He needed you more

We all have to die one day
It is sad to see them leave
Loved one, lost one
So hard to believe

"Word"
Is now just a memory
I miss you friend
And the pieces of your poetry

Let no selfish spirit haunt me
But a spirit of
It is ok
Let me not question your decision
But believe you when you say,
You are Savior

Trust was an issue
Anger was my past
When those things expired
You gave me new emotions
Hope, love lasts

We all have to die one day
It is sad to see them leave
Loved one, lost one
So hard to believe

Unbroken Bond

Why fight constantly?
Not forgiving,
Letting the years pass you by

Why concentrate on all the pain?
Letting the love slip away
It is hard to let go
Suffering
So you cry

It is a shame
Family,
Blood that runs through your veins the same
Somehow blood no longer bleeds
Not there for each other
Act like family is what you do not need

But sometimes family is all you have
Friends are not always there
But nowadays,
Family becomes like friends
Not there when you need them

So close,
It is crazy

The ones that are the closest to you
Hurt you the most

No matter the turmoil between
Still be willing to hold out your hand
Help the one in need

So many times people give with their hand still out
Expecting to receive something back
Why can't we give without the intention of getting?
How can we communicate without the intention of listening?
But we want everybody to hear what we have to say
Like it is all about us
We are so selfish

I heard someone say
It takes two to make a thing go right
All we want is love
But being vulnerable to love
Leaves us open to being hurt
Being broken

Hurt in ways that cannot be repaired
Or broken that takes time to heal
But nothing is impossible
Both sides must want to build
Mend any broken fences

We must have like-minded spirits to overcome the hurt
We must create a relationship that is still there for both

But the good thing about love
It is so patient, so kind
Family should be like love
Tight,
Un-messed with,
An unbroken bond

There Could Never Be Just One Thing

The one thing I love about You God
Is that You love me despite me
Man only loves a piece of what he sees
But God,
You have studied the core of me
Seeing the good and the ugly
You love me unconditionally
That's the one thing I love about You God

The one thing I love about You God
You are consistent in who You are
I had friends
Changing as if they were underwear
But that should have told me
How dirty they were

It's something how one minute
They want to be close
The next minute is filled with space
When something new comes around
But God,
I love the fact
You want to be close all the time
With You it's always intimate

The one thing I love about You God
Is that You are merciful
Never will You abandon or destroy me
Like man who gives up and kills so easily

The one thing I love about You God
You gave me Jesus
My Help
My Strength
My Shelter
In the time of storm
Who rebuked the wind
And to the waves
He said,
"Peace be still"
Instantly, things began to get calm
It's funny how man disobeys
But the sea and wind can listen
I am amazed!
There will never be just one thing I love about You
There are so many
You are everything
I cannot even dream of them all
You are so amazing

I am not worthy of all You have to offer
Or to know all You can do

But what I do know
Is enough
For me to want to worship
And give my life to You

I Met a Man

I met a Man
Yes, Lord
A Man
Holy and Divine
Quite spiritually fine
Knees dropper
Had to make Him all mine

I met a Man
One of a kind
I heard no one is perfect
But I think somebody lied

See I took the time to get to know Him
Did not judge so quickly
Instead I looked deeper
I could not find any flaws
Yet, I found more amazement

His mind is so creative
HE IS... deeper than poetry
When it comes to the word
HE IS... the originator of the story
Glory! Glory! Glory!

My Lord!
This Man
HE IS... everything
Yes sir
O, yes ma'am

HE IS... a giver
He stands with the perfect posture
Arms opened wide
Reminds me of the cross
There He was crucified
Laid His life down
Crown of thorns on his head
Clothed in a purple robe
Was slapped in his face
Pierced in his side
His blood I want to be covered with
So close I can taste

Following His orders
Being His slave,
I found salvation
He insured me with protection
He gets me
HE IS...
Understanding

I met a Man
Honest and patient
Kind and loving
Swept me off my feet
More of Him I am yearning

I pray that our spirits entwine beautifully
Let no one interfere with what we have gained
Satan I have abandoned
I found someone new
HE IS… the truth
Found love in romance

Once I gave him a chance
We danced
To sounds of melodies from heaven
Yes, I met a Man

You Are The Man

Your mind is brilliant
Your heart is gigantic
Your love has no comparison
You are on a whole new level of passion
You are romantic
Do without asking
You are the Man

You are the Man
Died on the cross
No one can keep You down though
You rise right back up

You are untouchable
Too Holy to break
You are unbreakable
You are the only one who can save the world
More than a hero
You are our Savior

Patient
I called that a waiter
You are the truth
Praises go up to You

Jesus to You I cling
Obeying whatever You command
You won't steer me wrong
With You I forever stand
Jesus, You
You are the Man

HE IS... Someone to Talk About

I never been the type to brag about a Man
But this Man
He's someone to talk about

Let me help you understand
See, how many men do you know that truly understands a woman?
Knows how to control their mood swings,
Turning their nagging into a closed mouth

See HE IS...
Mmmm
HE IS... Mr. Perfect
Make me feel like everything I been through is worth it
Because it led me to Him

He makes me so thirsty
And I hunger for His love
He is such a Gentleman
Opening doors
Walking side by side
I love for Him to take the lead
He's a better tour guide than I am

I am ok to be the follower
For once in my life
Because He IS… a real Man
No need to think twice

So used to wearing the pants in the relationship
Because men nowadays are weak
Tight pants, tight shirt
Don't want to be a man any more
But now I can put back on my skirt
Because I am with this new Man
Who has been after me since day one
Prior to this day
I use to take off and run

Have you ever had that one person that wanted you so bad?
Kept surprising
But you kept dodging
Kept pushing them away
But as you give in
You realize
It was the best thing that ever happened
No more worries
No more apologizing for the wait
Because this Man comes right on time
This man he knows how to put it down
Hold it down
Make me feel like I can trust again

One day,
I had an urge to be romantic
Feeling intimate
Didn't need any red roses, dim lights, or a candle
All I needed was Him
Any situation he can handle
Turning the knob on the tub,
Running water
Making me out of an example

The water we got in
Nice and warm
As he touches my body
Like I was his goddess
Rubbing against my skin
Soothing my soul
Washing away my sin

HE IS… so spiritual
Looks beyond my physical
He can do what no man can do,
He can work miracles

When times get rough
I would wonder why or how I made it through
Thinking it was luck

But I can see clearer now
Realized it was all a blessing
My lights are no longer flashing

So many seek
But never find
I acknowledge the fact
If I want change to come in my life
Something I must adjust
I figured it out
When I met this Man
That caused me to blush
This Man,
His name is
Jesus

Social Media

Hi,
I am the unknown
We never met face to face
But it is ok
I still know all about you
I read your post
Seen your pics
I clicked the like button quite often

Scrolling through your page
Mind blown from the filth
You throw a lot of shade
Your hands should be cramped
Typing away

You are your own match
Lit on fire
I see the good and the bad
Twisted desire
The pretty and the ugly
The intelligent and the illiterate
I see it all

Relationships crumble
Love falls

Real life partners are tuned out
When it comes to attention
Social media has it all

My God,
Why do you continue to give them love?
All they really want is likes
Why do you want their marriages to last?
When they don't even
Staying in the same home
Broken, inattentive
Zoned out
Letting social media control their life
Stealing the spotlight

It is all about logging in, posting pics
Addicted to the likes
Glued to cellphones
Stalking friends with quotation
Get a slight sensation of all the action

So many times I wondered,
Why are people so addicted to Facebook?
So I created a page
Logged-in to the depths of my cerebrum
Gently using tactics
Successfully getting to the bigger picture

Females with constant selfies,
I ask myself,
"Are they that into themselves, or is it insecurity?"
Waiting for someone to say they're beautiful
Seeking attention
Attraction is lost on the reverse side of the computer

Thoughts kept coming
Wondering,
How can a person,
With thousands of friends online,
Could be so lonely?

All walls are down
Everything is see-through
With an instant click
Private information is now public
It blows my mind
I am mentally exhausted

Seems like everyone is obsessed with the temporary
I am tired of reading life stories on the internet
Day by day itineraries,
Realize life has a bigger picture
Images of non-selfies
Illustration of the cross Jesus carried

Create a meme with words that say,
"I love Jesus because He died for me"
Now that is a photograph that should go viral
But most likely it would go unseen

Days are final
Lord be with us that we can see the importance
Not hungry for now
But greed for what is coming

One day turns into eternity
Let us be ready for the possibility
Today may be our last

Lord,
I pray we get in the habit
To spend more time with You than we do online
Let us embrace who we are
And love the one you designed

Be Who God Made

Say to yourself,
I am beautiful
I am smart
I am unique
Divine art
I am diamond jewelry
Yes, I bling
I am money
Cha-ching

I am a Christian
Sometimes I have a stumble in my walk
But I will never throw my hands up
I will keep Jesus in my heart

I am patient
I am kind
I am love
I will not be blind

I am faithful
I do not cheat
I do not lie
I am trustworthy

I am confident
I am whole
I am a hot commodity
I will not be sold

I am
And will always be
The person
God has made me

Wonderfully Made

God created you a woman
Bringing life from a man's rib
Not to take away, but to submit
Giving man the sight of preciousness

Understand that life is just a pine tree
You are that gift that is underneath
Wrapped in paper that is unique
Naturally, drawing eyes to seek

There is no need to degrade yourself
Hoping to find attention
With clothes that cover-up nothing
Showing off your crack
Believe that you are beautiful without cosmetic
Make-up is just that

Something that is made up
Covering up the insecurities
That remains an issue
Once the face that has been applied vanishes
It is a quick, temporary fix
Why hide your uniqueness?

Stop trying to cover-up the meaning of you

With blush, mascara, and eye-liner
Especially that cheap kind
That runs down your face
Let us embrace

The wonderfully made individual
You are art
That God has distinctively detailed with a brush
Keeping the perfect rhythm in his wrist
Bringing beauty to life
Patiently
No need to rush

Pay attention
You do not want to miss
The mystery that is inside
There you will find the prize
Where you will realize
God makes no mistakes

You are wonderfully made
Stop listening to society
Telling you what is the perfect shape
It is false accusation
Perfect is not what the world sees
Their image is just a personalized imagination

We are human
All have flaws
Unique
God designed us to be who we are

So that is why I,
I keep my head held high
No need for it to drag the floor
I walk with confidence
As I enter into the door
That God has opened up for me
Not afraid anymore

I close my ears to negativity
They say I have a long nose
But I say it is not long
It is just outstanding

See you cannot let people tear down your self-esteem
Trust me
People will try to bring you down,
Because they are broken down
People will make fun of you,
But the real issue is within themselves

I learned
When someone tries to judge me

Before they continue
I switch gears and say thank you
Because obviously I am on their mind
And they are jealous
Because I embrace the fact that I am wonderfully made

My soul knows well
Yours as well
So give thanks unto Thee
No matter how big or skinny
No matter the complexion or the accent
No matter what the world says
Love who you are and all you display
You were made with a purpose
Yes,
You are
Wonderfully made

My Identity

You can look me up and down
Or even sideways
You can call out my name
And tell me that I am lame
But God fabricated me
And I am not ashamed

You can try to label me
But my identity lies
In the hands of God
My identity has already been identified

I am that woman,
Crawling out of my Adam
Walking in the Garden of Eden
Naked
Clothes are irrelevant
There is nothing to hide
Myself,
I reveal
What is there to disguise?

I am an open book
Pages filled with my story
So read me

Instead of making an assumption
Twisting the truth into a lie

See we all become an Adam and an Eve
Being deceived
By a serpent
Knowledge grow on trees
There is where we get our discernment

Curiosity is our downfall
We want to know everything so urgent
Some things
We don't need to figure out or sample
That is why our laundry become so dirty
We need to clean up
God,
Please hand us the detergent

You can try to label me
But my identity lies
In the hands of God
My identity has already been identified

Do not tell me who I am
From what you think you see,
Do not jump into a pool
If you're not ready to swim deep,
Cannot spill the tea

If there isn't any,
You're not a judge
So stop judging me

You can look me up and down
Or even side ways
You can call me out my name
And tell me that I am lame
But God fabricated me
And I am not ashamed

You can try to label me
But my identity lies
In the hands of God
My identity has already been identified

I.D. me please
To see who I am
My name is unchangeable
I am God's child
Born out of destiny
Live on my knees
Praying to receive
All that is best for me

I was created on the day
Beauty was officially defined

I was thought of
The same time
God fashioned my mind

He never meant for me to stay in the form of a cocoon
God made me a grown butterfly
Flying to a different depth of life
Going through metamorphosis
Change of life

I am different than what you think you remember
Yes, I was heathen
O but now,
I am a Christian

I made it out of calamity
My old soul was taken
But I was given a better identity

You can look me up and down
Or even side ways
You can call me out my name
And tell me that I am lame
But God fabricated me
And I am not ashamed

You can try to label me
But my identity lies
In the hands of God
My identity already been identified

Confidentiality

Secrets kept
Safe in you
Weapons will not be formed against me
You made me bulletproof

I am confidential information
My soul I do not just hand out
I am a complex illustration
That only you can figure out

My soul is sacred
My soul is special
Cannot twist my mind off of God
I am not a pretzel

I am a tree
Growing tall
Rooted in the grounds of you
Strong I hold
So tight that no one can undo

Go green
Dare not to be blue
Anything is possible in God
Yes, HE IS… able

God's house has rules
That cannot be broken
To get in, there is a code
You must follow the words He has spoken

Heaven is above
Hell is beneath
Look up to the angels
And down to the thieves

Everyone is not about to see
The confidentiality in the spirit
There is limited access
So, I hope you got your ticket
There will only be a few

Secrets kept
Safe in you
Weapons will not be formed against me
You made me bulletproof

I am confidential information
My soul I do not just hand out
I am a complex illustration
That only you can figure out

Ebony

Ebony,
Be who God design you to be
Black is beauty,
An African American queen
Girl, you better love it
You are Ebony

Let us face it
Embrace it
Replace the negativity
Let us praise Him
For He made you differently

The best kept secret
You are what the world lust for
You are fortunate
Skin dripped in swag
Drips of chocolate
Blessed to be
Black is
Ebony

Ebony,
Be who God made you to be
Black is beauty

Skin deep
Inside image
Pictures worth a thousand words
So I guess it is vocabulary pricey
Let us face reality

Natural is in
So stick in the pick
And be you
Nappy roots
The story of the truth
Life of a black woman
Perms they turn to

Society thinks straight hair is important
But nothing is perfect
If everything was one way,
Then this life would be boring
Do you agree?
Beauty is in
And in is
Ebony

Black is back where you came from
You are the chosen one
A choice pick wisely
The love of brown skin

Love the skin you are in
Blessed to be
Black is
Ebony

Salute goes out to you
Balled up fist in the air
Show off your pride
Power to the people
A dose to prescribe

Medicate your mind
Realize
It is ok to be
Black is
Ebony

Life is a coloring book
Turned pages
See a few of you
So let us color you in

You are something to see
You are wonderfully made
You are unique
Cannot hide your style or your physique

Escape the chain and handcuffs of the world
And be free
Black is beauty
And beauty is
Ebony

Coffee Girl

Free to be
Me
That girl in a cup of
Caffeine
Mixed with hazelnut
Sugar
Coffee cream
I am a coffee girl
A brown, black bean

Get a mug
And appreciate
The taste of me,
I am hot
To your lips
Yes indeed

I am a coffee girl
Free to be
Me
That girl in a cup of
Caffeine
Mixed with hazelnut
Sugar
Coffee cream

I am a coffee girl
A brown, black bean

I am a coffee girl
Hot to your mouth
The talk is all about me
I am on fire
So please
Continue to blow
Rapidly
And put me out of my misery

For my master
I fein
Addicted to the Most High
I am a slave
God reigns

He designed me
With precision
Using a very exquisite technique
Loving the creation
I am not ashamed of me

I'm a coffee girl
Free to be
Me

That girl in a cup of
Caffeine
Mixed with hazelnut
Sugar
Coffee cream
I am a coffee girl
A brown, black bean

You can roast me
Until I am done
But God has the final say so
Cannot hold me back
I will cross the line to the punch
Laughter is good for the soul

Words we eat for lunch
Sometimes it can be so hard
That when we speak
You can hear us crunch

Talk is nothing but a coupon
Discounting intellect
Making intelligence cheap
Who cares if I am a coffee girl?
A brown, black bean
At the end of the day
I am still human
With feelings

See I am a coffee girl
Take me as I am,
Drink all of me

Open Your Book

Someone told me,
"If you ever want to hide something from a black person,
Just put it in a book"
Let that ponder in your mind
See the average black child
Does not see the highlights on the pages
Because their books are closed
Haunted by the openness
Do not want to be captured by the lames

But today,
The youth of all races
Turn their faces
Away from knowledge
In high school,
Not even thinking about college

Head is in the streets and sheets
Running high on mileage
Looking into mirrors
Only to exceed the expectations of the image they see on TV
While their brains are running
Running on E

They do not have interest in novels
I guess they judged the book by its cover
And got turned off by the preview
Got mixed in the trail
Going nuts like a cashew

A mind
They tell me,
Is a terrible thing to waste
Education is important
The key to success is knowledge
There is where power lies

Don't enslave your mind
Feeding it with things that are insignificant
Be all that you can be
Let go of the resistance
There is more to you than the streets

God clothed you not in a maybe
But a must
Giving you a defined existence
Everything he made
The Bible tells me,
"And it was good"
You are one of God's greatest creations

He is creative
You will never find him in the world of abbreviation
He continues to increase
Expanding this little old world
To a grandiose masterpiece

Stay in school
Open your book child
Enlighten your mind with information
So you can have an opinion
Letting your thoughts be heard
Open your book child

Do not be blinded by what is going on
Do not steal the words from man's mouth
Get to know for yourself
Before you wind up in an ouch

Be at the feet of Jesus
Every day
Asking him to lead the way
So you can follow
Asking him for a piece of mind
That has the desire for knowledge

Let you not be the next statistic
But the next standard

That makes a difference
 Let no man insinuate your future
But let God choose
For HE IS... the ruler

Do not enslave your mind
Feeding it with things that are insignificant
Be all that you can be
Let go of the resistance
There is more to you than the streets
You must believe

So stay in school
Open your book child
Enlighten your mind with information
So you can have an opinion
Letting your thoughts be heard
Open your book child

Every question deserves to be answered
Do not allow your thoughts to be buried in a pile
Just open your book child

Free-Dumb

Nothing can stop me now
I am gonna keep on walking
Keep on talking
Freedom don't fail me now

Blacks are bomb threats
Setting off alarms
People are untamed animals
Running wild
Intimidated by the mind of a black child

But we are enslaving our own mind
Holding it hostage from knowledge
They want us dead
So we fall in the trap
Killing up on each other

Freedom costs
Life is the fee
But I thought Jesus already paid the way
So, why can we not just be free?

Nothing can stop me now
I am gonna keep on walking

Keep on talking
Freedom don't fail me now

Signs to protest
No more silence
Let us speak out loud
Marching for freedom
Black was not made to be discouraged
So be proud

Yes, our skin is different
A worst way to say unique
But we are God's people
Not some kind of alien

It is not about skin
But what lies within
Skin is just a color
Eyes are damaging the mind
Maybe more people should be color blind

Freedom,
Does anyone know what it means?
Meaning no chains around the neck of a voice,
Around equal opportunity,
Around the word FREE-
DUMB are not we

Nothing can stop me now
I am gonna keep on walking
Keep on talking
Freedom don't fail me now

Freedom costs
Life is the fee
But I thought Jesus already paid the way
So why can we not just be free?

See this world is in desperate need of Jesus
We want to take Him out of everything
The main time we need Him
We want so much independence
That we even got loose from Jesus
That is not freedom

We hold ourselves to this small standard
Do not want to expand our horizons
Because old generations got into our minds
Telling us, "Blacks don't do this or do that"

If the sky is the limit,
How would we ever reach true success?
I know it is just an expression
But if we only reach for the sky,
How would we ever make it to heaven?

Just saying
Freedom costs
Life is the fee
But I thought Jesus already paid the way
So why can we not just be free?

Let's break the chains
Run to HE
Let's be FREE-
DUMB-DON'T BE

Unity

Bro. Johnny said,
"One plus one equals..."
It's simple as math
One plus one
Ummm,
What is that?
Some may need to pull out a calculator
Punch in the figures
The results may give you two
As Christians, we must get technical
Better yet, spiritual
It's a little more profound
Again
One plus one
He said the answer is one
You may be confused
In school
There are math books
Teaching us one plus one equals two
We all can believe that without questioning
But why when it comes to God, we argue?
Causing division in the church
The bible tells us there shall be no division
But yet we are so divided into two
Maybe it is flesh versus spirit

We should be united
Dropping titles of religion
There is only one
We should feel urgent to travel down one way streets
Not lanes that are merging
Making things beneficial to the way we want it to be
Lord, I pray to Thee
You give us the understanding of unity
Let us complete your joy by being of the same mind,
Having the same love
Let us be in full accord
Removing self from the picture
Making you our priority
You are the only one who can save our soul
Let us open up Webster
Become an inspector
Sometimes we need to look deeper into the word
Let us observe the definition of unity
The state of being united
Joined together not separate
But as a whole
Unity
We need more of it
Not just in the world
But mainly in the church
We are God's people
Supposed to exhibit His Word

Showing the lost ones how great is our God
So they will not think it is just another statement they heard
We should shine bright with love from the Son
We are unity
Meaning we are
One

God Is Not Man

Man
Easy
Breezy
Beautiful
Covered in the untruth
Hides evidence
What you see,
Is not always the proof

But God,
God will do what he says he will do
Numbers 23:19(NLT) says,
"God is not a man
So he does not lie
He is not human
So he does not change his mind"
That's Bible

But Man
Disguises
Gives birth to alibis
Promises are fumbled
Excuses are quickly thought of
When Man has failed to follow through

There will be a time to pay up
Bills are soon due

Judgment Day is coming
How long will your list be?
Of all the sins committed
Don't put your soul in jeopardy

Some people unconsciously volunteer their soul for Hell
It could not be me
I hate being hot
I cannot stand the heat

I have to start now
Getting my soul right
Because if I wait too late
Then it will ignite

God I want to be like you
I know I am Man
But I do not have to lie
Yes, I am human
But I need you to stabilize my mind

I see so many people
Cover-up the evidence of who they really are
Pulling others into their life
Without truly showing their world

Man
Easy
Breezy
Beautiful
Covered in the untruth
Hides evidence
What you see,
Is not always the proof

But God,
God will do what he says He will do
"God is not a man
So He does not lie
He is not human
So he does not change his mind"

Over It

Life was breathed into drama
No need to catch a fit
Wasting energy
Just be over it

Issues are issued out every day
You have to master the exhaustion
Life brings
Take precaution
Examine every circumstance thoroughly
To see if it is worth it
To be stressed out, mad, or should you just be over it

Some things are out of our control
We need to learn to relax in the arms of Jesus
He's the one who got our back
From the thief who stole
The precious gold
That was given by God

You cry until your eyes get exhausted
Every tear deserves to be wiped away
It is good to cover the wound with a bandage
Before it gets infected
The Devil will never stop coming
No matter how much you sit on a church pew every Sunday

He is constantly busy
Finding himself into your view
Causing you to lose focus
Losing site of the importance
Of the one you are trying to pursue

Do not give up so easily
The end of the fight is not due
The battlefield is always crowded
War is going on
There is nothing we can do
But pray

Why sit there in pity?
Shaking your head
You cannot resist the enemy
If you never turn the other way
And look to God instead

Issues are issued every day
You have to
Master the exhaustion
Life brings
Take precaution
Examine every circumstance thoroughly
To see if it is worth it
To be stressed out, mad, or should you just be over it?

Heart of Excuses

Stories told
Wasted lies
Wasted words
But no more
Truth unfolds

Paranoid
Constantly looking over shoulders
Watching, observing
A soggy heart
Soaked in excuses

It may dry and form glass
Can't hide from the reality
That it may break
It may crack
But you can still see through it

Pain is obvious
No matter how hard you try to disguise it
The hesitation of fear
Building walls of anxiety and insecurity

I was that student
In an incomplete classroom,

An imperfect university
Walking through the hallways of irrationality
Trying to make sense of the intensity
Pointing fingers
Coming up with more excuses

Read books on the mind
I learned how to lose it
Read books on the heart
I learned how to abuse it
Took loved ones for granted
They gave me a pass so I used it

Waste was made to flush
Sometimes it comes right back up
I see bathrooms as shelter,
A hiding place
Escaping the outside world
It is very misleading
A special room to get cleansed
Yet can be the filthiest place

I gazed into the mirror
That lies on the bare wall
Of that empty bathroom
Just that mirror and I
Alone

Communicated through the eyes
And there I stand

It was the first time I saw myself
A woman
Ready to give birth
25 years old
Ready to let go
Carrying a child for so long who is fragile
Hurt
Desperate for love
And is ready to come out

For so long, she has been locked up
Afraid to speak her emotions
Afraid to face her fears
But the woman in her is ready to hit it head on
Realize life is too short
Issues, it is time to get over and move on

Mirrors are the most honest
Reflection of the truth
Before, I lost sight of me
Because there, I morphed into you
Turned into someone I no longer recognize
Myself I barely knew

Drowned in your world
Suffocating in your presence
Yearning to be free from
Disappointment, failed promises, anger, deceit
Now I could only see me

My eyes are covered from the sight of you
No more excuses
No more blaming you for me
I am healed from hurt
Taking responsibility for my own actions and feelings

Tweaked my mind
I let go of hope in man
Attached myself to faith
What God has for me,
No one can take

I believe more in the unseen
What everyone else cannot see, I can
I learned to dig deep
In the heart of an excuse
I tucked it away
Now, I only pull out the truth

It Takes Two

Ecclesiastes 4: 9-12

Two are better than one, because they have a good return for their labor: If either of them falls down, one can help the other up. But pity anyone who falls and has no one to help them up. Also, if two lie down together, they will keep warm. But how can one keep warm alone? Though one may be overpowered, two can defend themselves. A cord of three strands is not quickly broken.

Some people think

They don't need anyone

I used to be that person

Thinking I can do it all by myself

And no wonder why,

I became so broken

Anger led me to believe

I only needed me

So I abandoned the world

And my past memory

I was cold

No one there to hand me a blanket

Life felt chilly

I was all alone

Every time I opened the pathway to my heart

It eventually closed

Was so tired of letting people in
So I began to slam doors

I was standing in the way
So I was unable to reach my breakthrough
Too stubborn to move
Couldn't even see the preview

Burdens were filled with a lot of heft
Carrying the weight on my shoulders
I didn't look out of my right eye
So everything seemed to go left

It's not a one man show
It takes two
Me and you
To make a thing go right
So let's collab
Building God's kingdom
Turning us two into a multitude
The more people
The less you will have to pick up on the tab

Where I fall,
I will never have to worry
Because I know you will be there
To pick me up

Where I lay,
I know I will never be cold
Because you will be there
Bundled up

It takes two
With the help of You, Lord
I know now
I will always need You

I put my guard down
I surrender
I gave up
Now, I give in
To You Jesus,
My dear friend

Trigger of the Gun

Hand is on the AK-47
What is stopping you from shooting?
There it is in your possession
Can you not see?
There is the Devil,
The murderer in the mirror
Running after you
So fast like he was running late on his curfew

If you let this man live
Then you will die
You might be scared to shoot the gun
But just pull the trigger
While closing your eyes

You have to do it fast
So you will not think about it
You will second guess yourself
But why are you doubting?

Just shoot!
It's either him or you
Which one will you rather choose… life or death?
Which one sounds better?

Do you want to win or lose?
Failing always leads to regret

See me,
I pulled the trigger of the gun
Nothing going to stop me from being with the Son
And I do mean
Nothing

So yes, I pulled the trigger
A spirit inside of me was running loose
So I grabbed it by the flesh
Introduced it to a noose
Excruciating pain was released from it
Like it was being induced
Speeding up the pregnancy
Give birth to brand new

Life Sentence

Sentence with a period at the end
I am done.
Punctuate next time with an exclamation point
Exciting, fun!

I am a murderer!
Did not shoot for the head
I shot for the soul
I wanted someone dead
Did not shoot for the head

Call me a gang banger
Hard as a big toe nail
Sharp as a Harvard student
Clever to speak unknown languages, fluent
Sharp as a Harvard student

All I hear is sirens
All I feel is handcuffs
All I wanted was love
My heart was broken
Along with my ego
Everything sucks, you know

Life sentence
I killed a man
When I went down to the watery grave of baptism
It was an old man
Needed to die anyway

The time had to come
Lord,
I am sorry for past sin
Lock me away in a heavenly prison

He was an angry man
His blood was boiling over
I tried to lower the temperature
I really did try
Instead, I marked my signature

Please listen
I felt threatened
My life was in danger
I did not know what I was up against
He was going to kill me
It was only self-defense

Read me my rights
Handcuff me to your body
I have no other choice

But to be your servant
Yes, I deserve it

Read me my rights
Judge me
I am ready to accept the charge
Sentence me for life
My name was forged
But now you see the real me

I want to have life in your prison
Yes, I want to live
Sentence me
You taught me about sacrifice
So, my soul I give

I would not have it any other way
Father, I am yours
Open the gates
I will walk in faithfully
Locking it back
Right behind me

Shattered Glass

I will never be
That same person
You have made

Disguising the beauty
That lies in the most sacred place of my naive eyes
Crying out with pity

Weeping
From the shattered glass
That has cut the palms of your criminal hands
From when you were breaking me

Robbing me of my joy
Exposing wounds
Stealing bandages
But now look who is bleeding

What comes around goes around
You will eventually reap what you are sowing
How dare you?
Mess with a child of God
And think you will get away with it
You have got to be kidding me
Bruises are temporal

Stains are those un-removable dimples
Cheeks are cheeky
Hiding the bright smiles
Only to advertise the sneaky grin
Creeping in

Slithering up the sleeves of the enemy
I have landed right where I was falling
I was in the position you wanted me
Stumbling over the works of God
Moving too fast just to get to you
I was clumsy

While you were pretending to be my friend
Ship I have ended
The boat has no more value after the crash
Smash the remaining of what we have
It will never be
The same

God,
Let me move on without thoughts of revenge
Give light to this tunnel of mine
Give back all that belongs to me
Let me no longer ignore the signs

Chains are chokers

Squeezing the life out of me
I am a Christian who was broken
Felt like I had nothing left to give
I was a broker

Now I am a breaker
Breaking the cycle of chains that had me tied up
I am free to be
The woman God designed so beautifully

My cheeks stopped being cheeky
My smile is as wide as it can be
Bright as the sunshine
My eyes are not naive any more
I have discovered what was disguised
Which was, life's beauty

Big mad is the enemy
To know I choose God
His Son I shadow
Trying to get close to Jesus
Preparing for the battle

My hands were cuffed
My feet were chained
My soul was strained
But I knew, I had something to change

Adjustments I made
Hell, I could not claim
Sin had to fade
I did not want to lie in the bed that I had made

So I got up
Washed my hands
Freed my feet
I can walk again
Heading to peace

Hearts on the table
Love I eat
I was plated a label
With words of defeat

I am undefeated
I cannot be beat
With God on my side
The adversary has no choice but to flee

I am who I am
My DNA is uniquely identifiable
I have a mind of my own
My actions, I am held accountable
Broken is fixable
So pick up that shattered glass

That has cut the palms of your criminal hands
And give it to God so he can piece it
Before it becomes inflammable

Big mad
Is the enemy
To know we choose God
His Son we should shadow
Trying to get closer to Jesus
Preparing for the battle

Seen a Demon

I have seen a demon
Veins lifted
Swollen from the blood
That was heavily pumping

Rising every morning
As if it was the sun
Hot to fire
A bullet from a gun

Startled me when I glanced in the mirror
Holding my chest
As if I had been shot
By my own reflection

Run!
Fast as you can
Sometimes the Devil wiggles his way inside
Trying to stir up some mess
Shooting at you
Sometimes it is hard to dodge the bullets

The serpent was my tongue
Sliding down my esophagus
Slithering through the highway of wickedness

Bible states that,
In the power of the tongue
Lies death and life
I was making funeral arrangements quite often
Killing people with harsh words
I was heartless

Inside was a demon
Running wild
Loose as a goose
Do not get me started
I did not want to stop
Until someone got, got

I have seen a demon
My eyes were lit with fire
Horns stuck out my head
I rolled with the Devil
Slept under sheets with him in my bed
Matching sleepwear in the color red

I have seen a demon
I was born of innocence
Pure
I was an angel
But then I started falling
Evil got in the way
Knocked me down

Until I started crawling
And found the strength to get back up

Anger was my downfall
Made it hard to find God
In the midst of the chaos
I was playing both sides
Greed made me want it all

One day a scripture hit me
Basically saying,
What is a man who has everything but loses his soul?
Honestly he has nothing at all

Father,
My mind is set
I heard when you rang the alarm
I am not going to hit snooze this time
I am going forward
Keeping you on my mind

Lord,
You gave me a second chance
This time
I am going to do it right
I am on your team to the end
Together we can make it to the championship
And win

Put My Name On It

Tags are for ownership
I claim
Tagging everything,
On it
I put my name

Overcame anger
It was you who gave me joy instead
Deliverance
On it
I believe it got my name

An old wall,
I took a sledgehammer
And beat it
Much deserving of a hit
There's a breakthrough
My name was tagged
With graffiti
Sprayed all over it

Tags are for ownership
I claim
Tagging everything

On it
I put my name

Wounds been covered,
On the cuts
You placed a bandage
Those wounds were open longer than they needed to be
But I was standing in the way of me
Sometimes we can be our own enemy

I say no more
Aboard the train
I'm gonna get mine
Not allowing another blessing to slip by

Tags are for ownership
I claim
Tagging everything
On it
I put my name

Salvation

Hit a 180
Not a 360
You will
Land where you fall

You better get on board
Before the door closes
He is coming back
Yes, Lord

If you are not riding with Jesus
Then you are rolling with
The one who wants your soul
To devour it

Get your head on tight
Screws are loose
Gotta be,
Why you would not want to follow the man of G.O.D?

You can be saved
Declare with your mouth
Believe with your heart
God raised Jesus from the dead
You too can be saved

Don't ever think
God gave up on you
Because of your downfall
The Bible tells me,
Every man sins and falls short of the glory of God
But it is by grace
You are saved by faith
Jesus see better for you
Than your own eyes

Study your Bible
Can you not hear the message?
Or, are you not feeling it?
What part do you not believe?
Maybe the part He died and was raised
See, It all started on that cross in Calvary

Let me be the mouth to tell the world
About the Son of Man
Give me the mind of wisdom
Heart of compassion
Ears to listen

Father,
Let the day come
Where they hear your word
And believe, repent, and confess it
Let them be ready to go in the water

The watery grave of baptism
Going down with the old man
Come up brand new
Your Son gave his life for us
Now it is time to give ours for You

Journal Pages

Journal Pages

Journal Pages

Journal Pages

Journal Pages

Journal Pages

Journal Pages

Journal Pages

Journal Pages

Journal Pages

Journal Pages

Journal Pages

Journal Pages

Journal Pages

Journal Pages

Journal Pages

Journal Pages

Journal Pages

Journal Pages

Journal Pages

Journal Pages

Journal Pages

Journal Pages

Journal Pages

Journal Pages

Journal Pages

Journal Pages

Journal Pages

Journal Pages

Made in the USA
Columbia, SC
30 January 2018